It's All About

OPTICS

How to Transform Your Wardrobe and Dress for the Job You Want

Miss Barbara ♡
Thank you so much
for always supporting
and encouraging me in
everything that I do. I
appreciate you so much!
I hope you love the book!

♡ Olivia Martz

It's All About

OPTICS

How to Transform Your Wardrobe and Dress for the Job You Want

OLIVIA A. MONTAGUE

Cover design by Rachel Montague

Printed in the United States

Visit us on the web!
www.styledbyolivia.com

For my Mom, Susan Honesty Montague, and Dad, Jonathan Montague, the epitome of style and class. Thank you for making me the woman I am today.

Table of Contents

Introduction

Style is a way to say who you are without having to speak.

-Rachel Zoe

Perception is reality. I've always loved that quote and it could not be truer. How others perceive you ultimately has a huge influence on how they interact with you, particularly in a professional environment. Your visual identity (how you dress) is one of the biggest ways to brand yourself, especially when it comes to your career. That is one of the reasons I have always loved fashion and styling. What you wear gives you the ability to introduce yourself without ever having to say a word. Visuals are a universal language that cross cultural and societal boundaries. Your clothing can be an extremely powerful tool to help elevate your career and confidence, if used in the right way.

If you want people to take you seriously, you first and foremost have to at least *look* like you take yourself seriously. Research shows that people form judgements about you within in the first 7 seconds of meeting you. Regardless of how intelligent you are or what type of person you are, people will form judgements about you solely based off of how you look. This is true in life and in business. Is it right? No. But it's the truth. Particularly if you're like me and work in an extremely competitive corporate environment. How you dress for the job matters. Regardless of what profession you are in, how you present yourself will have an impact on you in some way, shape, or form. Most people are too politically correct to tell you what everyone else is thinking and what everyone else has already learned. No one will let you know that wearing your club dress with a blazer is inappropriate and looks unprofessional. But they will all think it. Going into any work environment can be intimidating enough without having to worry about what to wear. Or worse, having to ask too many questions about what you should be wearing. When you walk into any professional setting I want you to have the tools you need to succeed.

With any job, and particularly in Corporate America, in order to be successful you have to know how to play the game. 50% of any job truly is learning to play the game. The other half is execution. I can say from years of professional experience in both New York City and Washington, D.C., that the quicker you learn the game, the sooner you'll flourish. Learning, growing, and getting ahead in this type of environment for the past five years has taught me so much about the importance of optics. You'd be surprised how much of an impact simply showing up, looking the part, and being on top of your game can have on your career. But one thing I've noticed is how much harder it can be for women in the workplace, particularly when it comes to dressing the part.

The amount of scrutiny that women face in society today is ridiculous. Everything from hair, to weight, to makeup is put under a microscope and held to impossibly high standards. It's insane and I wish I could say it stopped outside the office but it doesn't. Optics matter. There are just as many infuriating assumptions made about women in the workplace. I think many people assume, especially as women, just because you're a lawyer, entrepreneur, consultant, doctor, etc., that you're supposed to dress a certain way and that it can't be flattering. Or that you have to stay in a certain box when it comes to how you dress. Imagine a boring black or blue suit with kitten heels and a briefcase. I literally cringe just thinking about it. The narrative for women in the workplace has consistently been that dressing professionally or business casual means we have to look boring, overly preppy, or just generally uncomfortable. The message has been and continues to be that you can't truly dress how you want when in an office setting. In order to manage all of these unnecessary perceptions that people have of you, you must be deliberate with your appearance and how you dress. But the idea that in order for women to look professional they have to look boring is *done*.

Have you ever walked into a meeting and been nervous about what you're wearing? Have you ever been preparing for an interview and truly had no idea what is appropriate to wear? Have you ever had to ask someone if your dress is long enough or if it is appropriate for work in the first place? That's where this book comes in. The purpose of *It's All About Optics* is to teach you everything about cultivating a wardrobe that will help you to exude confidence in life and in any professional situation. My goal is to give you the tools you need to succeed in looking and feeling your best regardless of what you are wearing. This book will be your step by step guide to dressing like a professional and looking put together. Use the notes section in the back of this book to write down any ideas or inspiration that come to mind as you're reading.

I've worked in every type of professional setting you can imagine, from the halls of the Department of the Treasury, to Wall Street, to an interior design firm Georgetown, D.C., and everything in between. I learned early on that how you present yourself makes a difference. You don't have to look perfect, but you do have to look the part. Getting dressed for work or any occasion should not be a difficult process. Looking put together and stylish is not an exclusive right or only reserved for a privileged few. It's all about working with what you have and using it to your advantage. I am going to be brutally honest with you and give you every tip and trick I have learned. This book is a compilation of all the unwritten (until now) and nuanced rules of looking like a professional. It truly is all about optics.

CHAPTER 1

What You Have

Style is something that each of us already has, all we need to do is find it.

-Diane von Furstenberg

Personal style is like art. You have to start out with a canvas then build from there adding different colors. The same is true for your closet. You must first find your base then build from there, adding various pieces and accessories to create the perfect closet. Getting the foundation of your wardrobe established is one of the most important aspects of being able to dress both professionally and confidently. In order to get to that point, you first have to know what you have. You have to begin with clearing out all the unnecessary items, in order to make space for the new items. You also have to identify what your personal preferences are when it comes to your own style. Everyone has their own personal style, regardless of where you work or what you do for a living. This will be incredibly important later when I talk about dressing for the job that you want. In order to look and feel your best you have to know what your style is so that it can be tailored specifically to you. I promise it is easier than it sounds and I will walk you through step by step how to get there. Having a clear picture of everything that you have in your closet will give you a solid foundation to continue to build the wardrobe that you've always dreamed of.

Ultimately your closet is an investment. Have you ever sat down and really thought about how much money you spend on clothing, shoes, and accessories over the course of a year? If you're anything like me it can quickly add up. I remember once I had just bought the most gorgeous blouse with intricate lace detail along the sleeves. I promptly wore it, felt fabulous, then carelessly washed it and put it in the dryer with the rest of my laundry. The top came out of the dryer two sizes smaller and the lace detail matted and destroyed. I was devastated. Why spend all that money on clothes just for it to go to waste because I didn't read the wash instructions on the label? So obviously I figured it wouldn't happen again it was just a onetime mistake, I was "responsible" or something…until I did it again. I made the same mistake a few more times and ruined great pieces before it really hit me that I have to take care of my clothes if I want them to last. It also hit me that I can't afford to replace my wardrobe every month, so I had better get it together.

Knowing what you have in your closet will help you to realize what areas you need to work on while also helping you manage what you already own. There are parts of your closet that you probably don't even touch and there are also pieces in your closet that you wear every single week. The pieces you wear all the time, those will be the foundation for building your dream wardrobe. In order to get to that dream, you must first go through what you already have and decide what needs to stay and what fits into the personal style you've always wanted. That's the biggest part– being able to manage what you already have and learn what your style is, before you start adding more. There are 3 stages in order to get to that point.

Stage 1: Cleaning Out Your Closet

First and foremost, in order to maintain your closet you have to make sure that it's fully functional and that you are able to see and access all of your pieces. No more stuffing clothes into a drawer and never looking at them or hanging so many pieces in your closet that nothing else will fit. Your closet is a tool and it can be extremely helpful when getting dressed, particularly as a professional who constantly has to look put together. I'm always cleaning out my closet and using the methods explained below to have a wardrobe of cultivated pieces that I love and that work for my lifestyle. I do a full closet cleaning at least once every 6 months, and sometimes more often than that depending on how much I've been shopping. Having my closet clean and organized is the best feeling because I know that I will always be able to put outfits together in little to no time. In that aspect, cleaning out your closet will also help you to clear out some mental space. The thought of having to go through your closet should not be stressful, but I know for so many people that it is. It can definitely be an overwhelming task if you don't go in with a plan and that's where I'm here to help. There are five key steps to take when cleaning out your closet that will make it an

17

easier process. Take your time and really go through each step. It may not happen overnight and it may take multiple attempts, but I promise that getting past this first stage will be incredibly rewarding as you begin to transform your closet into the version you've always dreamed of.

Get Rid of Items You Haven't Worn in a Year

If you haven't worn a particular piece of clothing in over a year chances are you probably won't wear it again (at least not on a regular basis). I'm not talking about seasonal pieces, like your winter coat or bathing suit cover-up, just items in your everyday wardrobe. I know for me I used to always keep every old t-shirt, sweater, and cardigan in the hope that I would one day wear them again...and I never did. Getting rid of stuff that you don't wear is the first step to realizing what you have and maybe what you need to buy next time you go shopping. Be harsh with yourself during this step. Get rid of anything you have the slightest doubt about. You may want to keep everything or hold onto things you don't need, but just remember that transformation requires growth. You cannot stay the same and expect your life to change. Change is necessary in order to grow.

ACTION ITEM: Set a timer for 10-15 minutes and use this time to go item by item through all the items in your closet and any drawers that you have. Anything that has not been worn in a year goes. Repeat this step as many times as necessary.

After your 15 minutes is up, continue to go item by item through your closet and really analyze what needs to go. Make sure to give extra attention to items when you own more than 2 pairs. For example, if you have 10 pairs of jeans but you only wear 4 of them, you can probably get rid of at least 3 pairs of jeans. Be critical and really think about the impression that you want to give. Visualize your dream self. What are you wearing and how do you feel? As you go through your closet, if you find items that don't align with your vision of yourself, get rid of them. Remember the goal here is to have your closet reflect the best version of yourself...and in order to do that some pieces will have to go.

Keep, Trash, Donate or Sell

Deciding which pieces to get rid of can be difficult and may take multiple attempts. Don't get discouraged, you can do this. As you're going through your closet placing items in one of the following groups will help make this process much easier: Keep, Donate/Sell, or Trash.

Items in the KEEP pile are things that get to stay. These pieces made the cut. These are your go-to items, your favorite pair of jeans, that dress you always wear to happy hour, or that blazer you wear to meetings. Be extremely picky when it comes to your keep pile. These are the pieces that will be used to create your dream closet. Make sure that these are the items in your closet that you love and know you will be able to wear again and again. Items in the TRASH pile are self-explanatory. These pieces did not make the cut and will be thrown away. This includes anything with holes, broken zippers, irremovable stains, etc. The items you throw away are pieces that someone else would be unable to wear if you donated them. The DONATE or SELL pile will be donated or sold depending on your preference. When I donate clothing I usually give to Good Will or Salvation Army. But there are so many amazing organizations that need clothing. Below is a list of organizations that I regularly donate or volunteer with. You can also visit www.styledbyolivia.com/giveback to see more of my tips and suggestions on how to give back and donate your clothing in a responsible way. Giving back is one of the most rewarding things in life and having the opportunity to give back, even through clothing, is an amazing feeling.

Organizations to Donate Clothing

Dress for Success
www.dressforsuccess.org/get-involved

Good Will
www.goodwill.org/donate-and-shop

Salvation Army
www.satruck.org

....

PRO TIP: To get in the habit of not hoarding clothes and maintaining a healthy balance in your closet, whenever you go shopping or buy new items make a rule to give one piece away for every piece that you buy. For example if I go shopping and buy 2 new dresses for work, then I go through my closet and get rid of at least 2 pieces of clothing in my closet that I don't need. This will help you to gradually declutter your closet and really get rid of the stuff you know you don't need.

....

Another great way to recycle items in your closet that are still in new/good condition is to sell them. I'm always so surprised when people don't do this. It's such an easy way to make a few bucks and get money to put back into building your closet. I would definitely recommend Buffalo Exchange (www.buffaloexchange.com) and Plato's Closet (www.platoscloset.com). I have been selling at both places for years now and have had nothing but good experiences (although sometime they are kind of picky with what they accept so be aware of that). I also usually find great pieces to buy at both stores as well. I will discuss where I shop and my tips on shopping smart in Chapter 4.

If It Doesn't Fit, Get Rid of It

I know this sounds simple but I can't even count the amount of times I've kept something even though it didn't fit me. I would make excuses, "but it's so cute, I paid a lot for it, I'll lose weight and it'll fit again, blah, blah blah". Don't make excuses. If something does not fit you, get rid of it. Not fitting correctly includes items that don't make you feel good. Have you ever put something on and immediately felt horrible in it? Those are the pieces that need to go. Half the fun of getting dressed is getting to feel good about what you're wearing and how you look. If a piece does not make you feel good when you wear it that is reason enough for it to go. Getting rid of things that don't fit will make way for things that do. This will ultimately make your closet so much easier to manage.

Would You Buy it Again?

This is the ultimate question. Ask yourself this question when trying to decide if you should get rid of something or if you should keep it. If you walked into a store right now and wouldn't buy the item again then maybe you don't need it. This will help you to look critically at your closet and will ensure that it is full of pieces that you genuinely love.

Going through each of these steps will give you more space to begin to build your ideal closet. Don't get discouraged. To create the closet of your dreams you will need to let go of your current one.

Stage 2: Organize Your Closet

Now that you've cleaned out your closet, it is time to organize. And by organize I just mean group similar items together. All the coats go together, all the tops, blazers, dresses, etc. This includes organizing any drawers or additional closet storage you may have as well. This will make finding items so much easier. I cannot emphasize this step enough. Having a specific area in your closet for each type of item will help to save time whenever you have to get dressed. You will know exactly where everything is located and be able to get dressed faster and with greater ease. When my closet isn't organized it takes me forever to get dressed in the morning because I can't find anything. Especially now as a professional with a full time job and a business that I run, I do not have time to be late (especially not because of my clothes). When everything is organized by type it makes getting dressed that much easier because I know exactly where to find everything.

Where to Buy Closet Organization

The Container Store
www.containerstore.com

IKEA
www.ikea.com

Target
www.target.com

....

PRO TIP: Never underestimate how important hangers are to your overall closet organization. Invest in good hangers. I know it seems like a small thing but it truly makes all the difference. I recommend huggable hangers, they are what I have used in my closet since college and they are amazing. Basically these are the skinny velvet hangers that allow you to maximize the space in your closet and fit as much as possible. They prevent your clothes from easily falling off the hanger and will make your life so much easier. You can typically find them on sale (because I'm always on a budget) at TJMaxx but I have also found them at Target.

....

The overall goal of having your closet organized is to realize what you have in your closet and ultimately make your closet work better for you. There have been times when my closet wasn't organized and I actually forgot that I had certain pieces of clothing because I literally could not find them (sad but true). Now that I am in the habit of keeping my closet organized and regularly cleaning it out, not only does that not happen anymore but it also helps me to come up with better outfits. When I can see everything that I have it allows me play around with my outfits more and have fun with getting dressed. Having an organized closet make getting dressed every day that much better.

Stage 3: Identify Your Personal Style Preferences (and the Preferences of Your Job)

How you dress introduces you before you even say a word and even more so in professional settings. What type of message do you want to convey when you walk into a room? Do you want people to think you are professional, creative, outgoing, conservative...the list could go on and on. Knowing your personal and work styles will make getting dressed for any job, professional function, and life in general that much easier. It is also important to consider how you want to feel when you walk into a room. I don't know about you but whenever I walk into a meeting I need to feel confident and put together (at least on the outside). What styles of clothing make you feel the most confident? These are the type of questions you need to ask yourself as you are not only going through your closet, but when building your new one as well. The goal is for you to feel like the best version of yourself. This includes knowing what colors you prefer to wear. For me my go-to colors are black, white, and neutrals. Being in New York City for so long has definitely rubbed off on me, so I find myself wearing a lot of black (it really is perfect for any occasion). Because I know what works for me and for my job, shopping and creating outfits that I love is easier. I also know that for my industry, black, neutral colors, and collared shirts is what everyone wears. Alternatively, if you work in the fashion industry your wardrobe for work may be more a lot more creative and trendy. You could probably get away with wearing many different styles depending on your role. If you're like me and plan on working in the finance industry, your work wardrobe may have to be more conservative. Your closet will definitely include at least 1 or 2 suits and plenty of blazers.

The key to knowing how to dress in any professional environment is to do your research and learn as much as possible before you even arrive. Preparation is everything. Going on an interview is a great way to learn more about a specific company and how they expect employees to dress.

PRO TIP: When dressing for an interview I always dress business professional unless they explicitly say otherwise. That way when I show up, I am never be underdressed. It is always better to be overdressed than underdressed, especially during an interview. Being underdressed can give the wrong impression (i.e. I don't care about my image and therefore do not care enough about this job). I will go into further detail about how to dress professionally later on. You can also visit www.styledbyolivia.com/shop to download my free lookbook of interview outfits.

When you arrive for an interview at a company, take a good look around. What is everyone wearing? Is it more of a jeans and t-shirt place with a relaxed vibe, or a strict suit and tie atmosphere? Analyzing what other people are wearing will give you a good indication of the dress code. Once you have identified what the expectations are for whatever job you aspire to have, then you will be able to build your wardrobe from there. For example, if you know that you will need to wear blazers every Wednesday for your staff meeting, then you know you need to purchase at least 1 or 2 so that you are prepared. Focusing on what you have in your closet and what you need to add to your closet is all preparation so that you are able to face any professional situation dressed accordingly.

ACTION ITEM: Set a timer for 5 minutes and list the top 3 adjectives or phrases that you want people to think when they see you. Anything that comes to mind, write it down. You can use the notes section in the back of the book or keep this list in a notebook, planner or on a post it note. These are the 3 things that you will focus on when shopping for and building your professional wardrobe.

Knowing what you have in your closet is the first step to building a wardrobe that truly reflects your own sense of style. Going through each of these steps will not only give you a better idea of the clothing you already own, but will show you where your closet is going based on your style preferences.

Chapter 1: What You Have
Summary

....

Stage 1: Clean Out Your Closet

- Get Rid of Items You Haven't Worn in a Year
- Keep, Trash, Donate/Sell
- If It Doesn't Fit, Get Rid of It
- Would You Buy it Again?

Stage 2: Organize Your Closet

Stage 3: Identify Your Personal Style Preferences

Resources:

www.styledbyolivia.com/giveback

www.styledbyolivia.com/shop

CHAPTER 2

WHAT YOU NEED: THE BASICS

Simplicity is the ultimate sophistication

-Leonardo da Vinci

When I began my first corporate internship my first semester of college, I had no idea what to expect. I was moving to Washington, D.C. in a few months and I remember googling "business casual" and wondering how much a good suit was going to cost to me. What I needed, and eventually learned, was the basics. In order to build a solid foundation for your wardrobe you first need to master the basics then build from there. The basics are your bread and butter when it comes to your closet. These are the things that will help to enhance every single outfit that you ever plan to wear. These are the ride or dies. These are the things people who are seemingly always put together have mastered, and also the things most people never talk about.

Underwear, Undergarments, and Camisoles

First and foremost having the right underwear and undergarments will make a huge difference in how your clothing fundamentally looks on your body. Particularly in a professional environment, you can immediately tell if someone is wearing undergarments that are either unflattering or the wrong size. Especially when it comes to bras. I always recommend wearing a t-shirt bra when dressing for a professional setting. This means bras that are smooth and will lay flat under whatever it is you are wearing, even a t-shirt. I would stay away from anything with too much lace which can potentially show texture and may be too suggestive for work (save the lace for date night). When it comes to your career you want people to recognize you for the right reasons, like your ideas, work ethic, time management, not for wearing something inappropriate or provocative to the office.

So if you're anything like me when I first started my professional career, I barely had the right clothing let alone the right bras. This is where a good camisole (or tank top) comes in. Having a good black or nude camisole that you can wear under everything will make getting dressed for work so much easier. You can wear a camisole under almost anything, a dress, a button down, or a blazer. The possibilities are endless and it will easily pull together any look by giving you a smooth and even finish underneath your clothing. You can find really affordable great quality underwear and undergarments at Nordstrom Rack (www.nordstromrack.com). They carry amazing quality designer brands at a great discount. I will give you all of my tips and recommendations for where to shop on a budget in Chapter 4, Shop Smart.

PRO TIP: Get professionally sized for your bras. I promise it will change your life. My fabulous Aunt Judy took me on my first bra fitting after I graduated high school because I was so obviously wearing the wrong size. It was the most amazing experience because it truly helped all of my clothes to fit and look better (not to mention drastically improved my posture). Everything will look better on you if you are wearing the right bra. I recommend going to Nordstrom (www.nordstrom.com), the fitting is free and they have amazing customer service as well as a variety of price ranges. Once you know your size you can get resized annually or as necessary.

....

Pants and Jeans

Having 1-2 pairs of go-to work pants are a necessity when building your professional wardrobe. You cannot go wrong with a good quality pair of black dress pants. My preference is black because of the versatility and ability to mix-and-match easily. They will go with any outfit and will require little to no effort when getting dressed. You can wear black pants with any color and thus wear the same pants multiple times in a given week. Having pants that are practical for your job will save you both time and money. If you want to see different ways to style black dress pants, visit www.styledbyolivia.com/shop to download my free business casual and professional lookbooks which include pictures of multiple outfits with black pants.

Having a go to pair of jeans is equally as important as having dress pants in my opinion. And let's be honest a good pair of jeans can make you feel amazing. You should have at least 1 pair of jeans that can be dressed up or down depending on the occasion. I personally do not work in an environment where jeans are acceptable, but that is not true for every company. Some companies have a more relaxed dress code where jeans can be worn every day. Having at least one pair of nice jeans in your closet will ensure that regardless of the work environment, you will be prepared.

PRO TIP: Buy an iron. You need it. The last thing you ever want to do is show up to any job looking wrinkled. It gives the impression that you are not put together. If you are sloppy in your appearance then you could also be sloppy in your work. In order to consistently look polished make sure to iron any wrinkled pieces prior to wearing them. If you don't have an iron right now, hang wrinkled shirts or pants in the bathroom while you take a hot shower. The steam from the shower will help to remove the appearance of wrinkles.

....

Shoes

Shoes can make or break an outfit. There are 2 basic type of shoes that every professional should have in their closet. It will make the process of creating outfits for work much easier when you have the right shoes. Remember these are just the basics, if you are just starting your professional career or want to evolve the way you dress for work, these are the 2 pairs of shoes you need in your closet.

Flats

Every professional needs a pair of simple flats in a neutral color (black, brown, grey, nude, etc.). Neutral colors go with everything so you won't have to worry about matching your shoes with your outfit. The goal is to make the process of pairing your shoes with your outfit easy and straight forward. One pair of flats minimum is my suggestion. Remember this is just for the basics, I personally love red flats as a way to add a pop of color to any outfit (especially since I always wear black). But when you are building the foundation of your professional wardrobe, a black pair of flats will be invaluable. A simple pair of black ballerina flats will go with any outfit and will save you time when deciding what shoes to wear.

....

PRO TIP: Buy liner socks. Sometimes flats can hurt your feet or even give you blisters. To avoid this make sure to purchase liner socks. These are the extra low cut and thin socks, typically with grips on the bottom, that are made specifically for wearing with flats and heels. You can purchase liner socks online or in any department store in the sock aisle. Your feet will thank you.

....

Heels

I was once asked in an interview what makes me feel powerful. I responded without hesitation, "a great pair of heels". Everyone needs a pair of neutral color heels. And I'm not talking about the heels you wear to the club. A pair of heels that are 3-4 inches is ideal for a professional environment and can help to dress up any look. Heels force you to stand taller, walk straighter, and overall change the way you carry yourself. For me, whenever I have an important meeting or know I will be meeting with clients, I wear heels. I know heels can be intimidating and are difficult to walk in for many people. Practice walking around your house in heels just to get used to the feeling and walking with composure. Keep practicing until you feel confident.

....

PRO TIP: When buying black shoes for work, go for patent leather. Patent leather is easier to clean and maintain than leather. Plus, it will always look like you polished or cleaned your shoes, which immediately makes you look more put together.

....

Another important aspect to remember when it comes to heels is that most women don't wear them for the entire day (myself included). I rarely wear heels to the office or even to an event. If I do, 9 times out of 10 I was wearing flats the entire day then switched to my heels right before

39

I walked into the event. I'll wear my heels to a meeting then change into my flats while I'm working or out in the city. There is no way I would ever be on time if I had to rush through the subways of New York in heels. Save yourself, and more importantly your feet, and always bring a pair of flats with you when you plan on wearing heels.

PRO TIP: Take your shoes to a cobbler. I can't even count the amount of shoes I have ruined in New York City. From broken heels to ruined leather. Life can be hard on your shoes so if you ever need to get the heels of your shoes repaired, take them to a cobbler. Just google 'shoe repair' in your area and a list of places should come up. Having a go to place where you can get your shoes fixed will make your professional life that much easier.

Bonus: Boots

I think it's also important to mention boots and booties, especially if you live in a place like New York City which can get cold. Boots are the perfect option for still looking put together without being cold. A simple pair of black or brown booties will be invaluable if you live in a place that gets cold during the winter. Boots with a reasonable heel or no heel at all will be easiest to transition into an office setting.

To see examples of work appropriate shoes, visit www.styledbyolivia.com/shop to download my free work shoes guide.

Keep it Simple: Accessories, Jewelry, and Looking Put Together

Always keep it simple with you accessories and overall look when first learning to navigate a new or unfamiliar professional environment. It definitely takes time to learn about your surroundings. Give yourself time to learn and grow in this new place, to see where you fit in and how you can still be yourself while having an image you can be proud of. I don't want you to think I'm saying everyone should be a cookie cutter version of themselves or that you have to wear the same thing as everyone else in your office. Wear what works for you and your visual identity, always while being aware. I think awareness is such an important trait to have as a woman in any professional setting. But it is important to still feel like yourself when you come to work and incorporating your own personal sense of style into your work wardrobe will help with that. So wear what you feel comfortable with but remember to keep it simple.

PRO TIP: Always get your nails done before going on an interview. Never show up to an interview with chipped nail polish or dirty nails. Regardless of what industry you are going into this does not make a good impression. Especially when you are in the interviewing stage, having your nails done is an easy way to instantly look put together. I recommend a light or neutral color.

If you are going into a corporate environment wear minimal jewelry that is not distracting in any way. Do not wear bright hot pink hoop earrings or a 20 bangles that all make noise when you move. As a general rule, you should not wear any accessories that make a lot of noise. If you're starting a new job and aren't sure about what to wear...less is more. While you're still getting adjusted to the new environment I recommend keeping it very simple and wearing a studs with a watch or bracelet until you see what is acceptable. For me, because I have to make so many decisions in any given work day, I don't like having to think and make decisions about my accessories for work. Because of this, I have a go to handbag and set of jewelry that I wear every day with slight variations if I really want to switch things up. I wear a pair of stud earrings, Pandora bracelet, ring, and sometimes a watch every day. The earrings or bracelets may change, but this is the jewelry that I wear on any given work day. Having this set formula for what I'm going to wear makes getting dressed so much easier. If you are in a corporate environment I would recommend having a simple go to set of jewelry that you wear. This will effortlessly make you look more polished and put together. Aside from jewelry, there are 3 key accessories that I have found will only enhance the look of any professional.

Belts

Having at least one belt that perfectly fits your waist is a must. I know one problem I frequently have with both dress pants and jeans is that they will fit perfectly on my legs but the waist will be too big. This is where having at least one go-to belt will be incredibly helpful. I would recommend getting a belt in a neutral color such as black or brown so that you will be able to wear it with any outfit. My current favorite belt is one that I found on sale at H&M for $6.

Work Bag

Having a ride or die handbag that you know can handle being thrown around will make your life easier. Working in New York City is incredibly rough on my workbags, from the subway, meetings, clients, and everything in between. Work bags typically get pretty beat up so having a designated bag that you are ok with getting over used is a must. The one bag that I have consistently used for work since college, and highly recommend for any professional, is the Longchamp Large Le Pliage tote. You can fit your entire life and then some in this bag. It is the perfect bag for work and will last you for years.

Watches

A watch will be incredibly valuable as you begin your professional career. 9 times out of 10 it's not appropriate to (openly) be on your phone during business hours.

Having a watch will make it easier to quickly check the time and help with time management. It doesn't need to be an overly expensive or flashy watch. It should actually be something simple and classic that will work with multiple outfits. Having a watch is always an asset.

Fit and Size

Have you ever put together an amazing outfit, only to put it on and realize that the fit is completely off? The fit and size of your clothing matters just as much as the clothing you decide to wear. There are some stores I will not buy anything from unless I can try it on because I know the fit is completely off. Don't get caught up in the size. What matters is that your clothing looks good on you and that you can feel comfortable and confident. When in doubt go for the correct fit, do not worry about size.

When it comes to your clothing for work or a professional environment, it should never be tight. Overly tight clothing in a work setting can be seen as unprofessional and again may give you attention for the wrong reasons. You never want to be a topic of discuss at the office because you wore something inappropriate. If a piece of clothing is too tight across your chest or butt, do not wear it to the office. Yes people will notice and it will not be positive. If you could wear it to the club, you cannot wear it to the office. Do not try and put a blazer over a bodycon dress and think that no one will notice. I once had a manager who told me when she started working she just transitioned her closet by wearing sweaters over dresses and skirts she wore for a night out. I was visibly horrified. Especially if you work in a corporate setting, do not wear bodycon dresses or skirts to the office. As I mentioned before, you should do research on the type of work environment you are in or will be entering to know what is appropriate and what is not. But as a general rule, tight clothing that purposefully accentuates your curves or cleavage is not acceptable.

PRO TIP: Try your clothing on before you make a purchase. I know it can be tedious and annoying but it will save you time and money in the long run. What's the point of buying something only to realize later once you get home that it doesn't fit? Obviously this isn't always possible but when you can, try on all potential purchases.

Having a strong grasp of these basic concepts will make any outfit that you create look put together. Looking professional has nothing to do with wearing overpriced, uncomfortable, or designer clothing. It truly is about optics and putting your clothing together in a way that portrays a positive image. Combine your style with the basics and you will notice a transformation in how you dress.

ACTION ITEM: Use the Items to Buy table on the next page to create a list of the top 10 pieces you need to add to your wardrobe. Really think about what fundamental pieces you are missing and what your closet needs. This table will help you to focus as you begin to shop for new items.

To download the table visit
www.styledbyolivia.com/shop

Items to Buy

Chapter 2: What You Need

Summary

....

The Basics

- Underwear, Undergarments, and Camisoles
- Pants and Jeans
- Shoes
- Accessories
- Fit and Size

Resources:

www.styledbyolivia.com/shop

CHAPTER 3

SHOP SMART

Price is what you pay. Value is what you get.

-Warren Buffett

How you shop is a key part of making your closet transformation a success. As you know, I work in the finance industry and also happen to be a huge personal finance nerd. The LAST thing I ever want to do is waste money or not get the optimal benefit and value from the money I do spend. In order to do that there are specific guidelines that I follow whenever I go shopping for clothing, accessories, or anything for that matter. Becoming more disciplined with my money has not only made my closet better, but it has also helped me to reach my financial goals quicker. I used to make the mistake of going shopping without a plan a lot when I first got to college. I would always buy stuff I didn't actually need because it was on sale or I thought it was cute at the time. I quickly came to my senses when I realized how much I could be saving if I just changed my approach. Having a specific strategy that you use before you do any shopping will help to make sure you are always making smart decisions before you add anything to your closet.

Have a Goal

Goal setting is a key component to success, not just with your wardrobe, but in life. How are you supposed to know where you are headed if you don't have a goal? Before you leave to go shopping make a list of what exactly you want or need to buy. Now that you've cleaned out your closet you will be able to see exactly which areas of your closet need the most attention. Do not go shopping without a specific goal in mind. "I need to find 1 pair of black jeans and 3 shirts that I can wear to work" is a specific goal. "I want to find something to wear to work" is not. Make your shopping goals clear and specific. I've lost count of the amount of times I've gone shopping looking for one specific item and because I got so *caught up* in shopping, I failed to get the one thing I actually needed. Not only does this waste money but time as well. Save yourself the headache and always go into any shopping situation with a clear and specific goal.

PRO TIP: Always shop during sales. I know this sounds simple but it will help you so much in the long run, especially if you're like me and on a budget. One way to stay on top of when sales are happening is to follow your favorite stores on social media. Most stores announce their sales ahead of time on Instagram, Twitter, or Snapchat so following them will definitely give you a heads up for when to shop. I've also noticed that a lot of stores will offer exclusive deals and discount codes to their social media followers, so be on the lookout for that.

Budget

I cannot stress the importance of having a good budget. My budget truly changed my life and my ability to live the life of my dreams (and I'm not even being dramatic). Having a budget and then incorporating shopping into that budget will help you to get more out of your shopping experiences. Working in finance and just being a general personal finance nerd has had such a huge impact on how I think about and manage my money. Like I said before, I don't like wasting my money. I like to know exactly where my money is going and that I am on track to reach my financial goals. I really enjoy traveling regularly and I plan on owning my own home in a few years. That will not happen if I spend my entire paycheck at the mall or on a handbag.

You deserve to have the closet you've always wanted and a budget will help you to do that. If you know that it will cost roughly $500 to redo your entire closet then you can start to plan and budget for that now. Patience is always the key when it comes to budgeting and reaching your financial goals. It will not happen overnight, you will not wake up one morning and magically have a perfectly balanced budget with hundreds of dollars to redo your closet. But it's really important to remember that you can do it one step at a time. It's possible. You just have to start and then little by little you will reach your goal. If you save $10 every week for an entire year, by the end of the year you will have saved $520. Having a budget isn't supposed to be some miserable experience, so please do not stress yourself out. It's really just an amazing tool to help you reach your full potential. It definitely takes some getting used to but I can promise you that it will be worth it. The discipline that you develop from having a budget will transform not just your closet but your life.

PRO TIP: Always have a set amount you are willing to spend before you start shopping. This is what always used to get me. Give yourself a limit BEFORE you go shopping for anything. If you know that you can only spend $50, then that will help you to stay on track but will also help you figure out what you can actually afford. It's all fun and games until all of your pending charges hit your checking account at the same time. Do yourself a favor and always set the amount before you shop.

....

Limit Splurging

Limiting big purchases really forces you to really focus on what you need. I typically only splurge on items at most once a season, depending on how I'm doing with my budget. One year in college it was a Zara camel coat (and I still wear the coat to this day). Another year it was a designer handbag I had wanted for years. I know since I only get one big purchase every so often I want it to be on something practical that I love, while also getting my money's worth. This also helps me to save money because I'm not constantly shopping or wasting money on expensive items that I don't really need.

....

PRO TIP: Buy used and preloved items. One of my best friends has a rule, "I never pay full price", which is the perfect attitude to have when shopping. There is no reason to pay full price for items that you can find somewhere else for a discount. This is particularly true when it comes to luxury and designer pieces. I personally love Fashionphile (www.fashionphile.com) for preloved luxury items mainly because they allow you to pay for pieces in installments. This works great with a budget because you can space a large purchase out over multiple weeks. I do not recommend paying full price for everything in your closet; it just isn't practical. Find outlet malls in your area, consignment shops, and know when sales are happening. There are so many different ways to avoid paying full price. Find one that works for you.

Process of Elimination

One of my favorite techniques to use when shopping is the process of elimination. If you're like me, love to shop and can sometimes get carried away, then this is a great technique to use. Whenever you go shopping, have a goal, and pick up all of the pieces you like or think would fit into the image you want create for yourself. Anything that you immediately love or something you think would be the perfect fit in your closet, pick it up. Be sure to check the prices as you go, and immediately put back anything you know you can't afford.

PRO TIP: When online shopping, always be aware of all return policies before you make a purchase online. This is one of the reasons I love ASOS and Nordstrom, both offer free return shipping on all orders. Always check the return policy before you buy anything online.

Now that you have all the pieces you know you love (and for me this is usually a ton of unnecessary stuff), go piece by piece and decide what to keep. My usual rule is that if I can't think of at least 3 different outfits or ways I could wear a certain piece then I probably won't wear it often enough for it to be worth buying. And be brutally honest with yourself, if you know that you already have 5 pairs of jeans, chances are you don't need another one. Doing this step anytime I go shopping has helped me to make better decisions and only buy pieces I know I will wear.

PRO TIP: Baby your clothes. Like I've said before, I treat my wardrobe as an investment and I want to get the biggest return that I can from my investment (aka I want my clothing to last as long as possible). I always make sure to read the care instructions before I wash anything, just to make sure washing it won't ruin the piece. Also, having special items dry cleaned is a great way to further preserve the life of an item.

Another important step to take when shopping is making sure that the pieces you do decide to buy are versatile and can be worn in multiple different settings. For me this means buying pieces I know I can wear to work and also in my everyday life. You don't want to have a closet full of "boring" work clothes that you never want to wear. The whole point of redoing your wardrobe is to have pieces that you genuinely love and make you feel like the best version of yourself.

Where Do I Shop?

....

These are the stores that I have used for years to build my wardrobe into what it is today. This list continues to grow and evolve so visit www.styledbyolivia.com to keep up with all my current recommendations.

ASOS: www.asos.com

Buffalo Exchange: www.buffaloexchange.com

Century 21: www.c21stores.com

Fashionphile: www.fashionphile.com

LOFT: www.loft.com

Nordstrom: www.nordstrom.com

Nordstrom Rack: www.nordstromrack.com

Plato's Closet: www.platoscloset.com

TJMaxx: www.tjmaxx.tjx.com

Zara: www.zara.com

Chapter 3: Shop Smart

Summary

....

Shop Smart

- Have a Goal

- Budget

- Limit Splurging

- Process of Elimination

Resources:

www.styledbyolivia.com/shop

CHAPTER 4

DRESS FOR THE JOB

I never dreamed about success.
I worked for it.

-Estee Lauder

Between working in two of the most powerful cities in the world, Washington, D.C. and New York City, the one thing I have noticed most about the successful women around me is that they all have a strong and purposeful image. They dress with intention. What they stand for is communicated every single day, not just through their work but in the way that they dress and carry themselves. This approach and mindset to getting dressed is the key to looking your best. You have to dress on purpose and know that optics matter. Let's be real, life is busy enough as it is without having to worry about what to wear. If you develop a set wardrobe and standard for how you are going to look, then you will eliminate the amount of decisions required to get dressed.

In order to be taken seriously you need to dress like you take yourself seriously. This is true in any professional setting and especially when making lasting impressions. I've seen women who are managers be mistaken for assistants simply because of the way that they were dressed. As a woman this annoys me, but as an image consultant it is even more infuriating. No one should ever assume you are under qualified because of what you are wearing. Period. But the reverse can also be true. Dressing well and developing what they call "executive presence" can immediately help to improve your credibility. What you wear has power and how you present yourself in your professional environment matters. This is incredibly important even if you are an intern. You would be surprised at how much people talk about and criticize when interns dress inappropriately.

Whether you are just starting your career or have been working for years, how you dress has an impact on how you are perceived. Maintaining a professional appearance will set you apart for all of the right reasons.

To build a professional and polished look, you must pair the wardrobe basics we just covered, with your own sense of style. That mixture is what will cause you to look put together in any setting. As I mentioned in Chapter 1, regardless of where you work, everyone has their own personal style. I don't want you to think that just because you want to transform your closet and have a more professional look that you can't still be yourself. This could not be further from the truth. You are simply becoming and even better version of yourself. The goal is to combine the solid foundation you've built in your wardrobe with professional pieces that reflect who you are and what you represent. You have to dress with intention and the more you do it the easier it will become.

So what does looking like a professional really mean? You will hear a lot of people talk about business casual, business professional, and my personal favorite (just because I think it's hysterical) business appropriate. All of these things are more or less trying to convey the same idea – there is a standard for how you should dress for your job. Once you learn the different standards then you will be able to create outfits that send the right message and give you a positive image.

The Difference between Business Professional and Business Casual

What exactly is business casual and how does it differ from business professional? This is a question I get a lot and it can be confusing, particularly if you have never worked in a corporate environment. Business professional is typically what you see lawyers, bankers, and congresswomen wear. It is a very conservative look and can be categorized by suits, ties, and collared shirts. The suits are typically black, dark navy, or grey. The collared shirts are typically white or light blue. Business professional shoes are always closed toe such as heels, flats, or dress shoes and are usually in a neutral color like brown or black. These are all staples when dressing business professional. Business casual is more relaxed but is still considered conservative. Business casual is typically what you see in most office settings. This includes sweaters, khakis, dress pants, blouses and maybe even jeans depending on the environment.

Business casual shoes can be closed toe or open toe depending on the company and may even include sandals or sneakers. And I know what you're thinking...how boring. But it doesn't have to be. It really is all about how you bring the right pieces together in a way that is still appropriate but fun. To see detailed pictures of business professional outfits and business casual outfits, visit www.styledbyolivia.com/shop to download my free Business Professional vs. Business Casual lookbook.

The key in any professional setting is to be aware of your surroundings and what is considered appropriate. Start out conservative when you're just learning then branch out as you get more comfortable. Your clothes are an amazing form of self-expression and you should enjoy getting dressed every day.

Key Pieces for Any Professional Wardrobe

When dressing for the job that you want, the pieces I outline below are items that will enhance any professional wardrobe. These are the pieces that you will gradually add to your wardrobe over time. They will be unique to you and will become a key part of branding yourself. Take for example the iconic Coco Chanel. She is known obviously for her incredible fashion empire, but also for her signature looks of all black, tweed jackets, and pearls. As you begin to visualize how you want to dress for work, think of subtle ways to show your personality through your clothing. For me I love classic and feminine silhouettes, yet still conservative and professional. So I gravitate towards looks that portray that style (think Michelle Obama). This is the fun part where you let your personality shine through in different ways.

Blazer

Regardless of your profession everyone needs a good blazer. It doesn't matter where you work, a good blazer can automatically dress up any outfit and make you look more put together. I recommend a blazer in a neutral color, such as black or grey, if you are just starting out in the professional world or if you're redoing your wardrobe. I like wearing blazers with a white t-shirt and skinny jeans or khakis depending on the type of environment. A blazer in a neutral color will be incredibly versatile and allow you to get your money's worth. I will talk about this more later but getting the most out of your clothing is an incredibly smart financial move and should always be the goal whenever you shop.

....

PRO TIP: Make sure that your blazers are long enough and fit properly. This is one of the most common mistakes I see when it comes to blazers and professional attire in general. Your blazer should not be tight across your shoulders and should come to at least your hips in length. There are so many different types of blazers, I recommend trying on several different types so that you get an idea of what looks best on your body type.

....

Pencil Skirt

The pencil skirt is a classic piece that is incredibly versatile, especially in the color black. A black pencil skirt will go with everything. Paired with a loose fitting blouse, it is a classic and polished look that will take little to no effort. High waisted pencil skirts can be extremely flattering and classic if worn in the right length. In an office setting, your skirt length should always come to your knees or lower. Do not EVER wear a skirt that is above your knees without also wearing opaque tights. The office is never the place for a mini skirt if you want to be taken seriously. This is a common mistake I see interns make, wearing skirts that are entirely too short or too tight. Always think back to the image that you want to portray and if a particular piece fits into the visual identity that you want.

....

PRO TIP: Invest in multiple pairs of tights. You can find tights at any department store for only a few dollars. As a woman in the finance industry, I wear tights regularly especially when the weather is cold. Having several pairs of tights in your closet will make getting dressed so much easier. I typically wear black tights with everything from dresses to pencil skirts. If you have a dress that you are worried may be too short for the office, try pairing it with black tights. I've learned that black tights can help to give most dresses a more conservative look.

....

Statement Coat

A statement coat is a necessity when dressing professionally during the colder months. This is only applicable if you live in a place that experiences cold weather. I recommend an oversized structured coat which will still look great with multiple layers. Dressing professionally during the colder months can sometimes be a challenge. But if you have a coat that automatically pulls your entire look together, then getting dressed will be that much easier.

PRO TIP: Go up a size when buying coats. This is a problem I came across early in my career. I would have a fabulous outfit, suit, heels, the works…but my coat would be too tight when worn with a suit jacket. If you typically wear a small, go up a size and get a medium. Going up one size will allow you to wear bulkier items while still comfortably wearing your coat.

Sweaters, Blouses, and Shirts

Sweaters will become your best friend when you begin to dress for the business world. My go to look with sweaters is black dress pants, a black camisole, and any color sweater. It takes me less than 2 minutes to put this type of outfit together and I know that I will automatically look put together. I recommend having at least two sweaters that you know without a doubt will look great on you. Having multiple looks that you know work well together will again cut down on the number of decisions you have to make when getting dressed. The goal is to make the process of putting together professional looks second nature so that you eventually do not have to think about it.

Similar to sweaters a good shirt or blouse will come in extremely handy when dressing business casual. They can be worn on their own, under sweaters, and also under blazers. I suggest getting shirts in white or neutral colors so that they can go with everything, which again will makes getting dressed so much easier. A white or light blue collared shirt are also signature pieces in most professional closets. You can't go wrong with a white collared shirt, black pants, and black pumps. And depending on what type of work environment you are in, a nice blouse can also be worn with skinny jeans and still look very professional. The goal here is to give yourself options that can be worn multiple ways. For example, a blouse that can be worn with dress pants, jeans, or a pencil skirt will be easier to style and incredibly helpful when putting together outfits.

The Little Black Dress
(and Every Dress You'll Ever Need)

You cannot go wrong with a little black dress. It is a classic and timeless look in any setting. The little black dress is so famous because it is such a versatile option for everyone. You can dress it up or down and look amazing either way. Especially if you are in a corporate environment where business professional dress is required, I recommend having at least 2 different black dress options.

A little black dress is also perfect for transitioning from work to an after work event. I know a lot of professionals who deal with the issue of transferring an office look into a look that will work for happy hour, dinner, or an event after work. The little black dress, and any statement dress really, is the perfect option. A statement dress is a piece that defines your personal style and is a complete outfit all on its own. A statement dress is the perfect way to look like you put effort into your outfit when really it takes none at all.

Dresses in general make getting dressed easier because they take away the amount of decisions required to put together an outfit. Without a doubt my favorite type of dress is the midi dress. A midi dress is a dress with a longer hem that comes below the knees but above the calves. I cannot say enough good things about midi dresses because they are just so easy. Especially on those days when you just really don't feel like trying, midi dresses make it look like you put a lot of effort into your look. Anything that automatically makes it looked like I tried, especially when I didn't, is a winner to me. The silhouette is also very flattering on so many different body types. This is the perfect grab-and-go type of outfit for any wardrobe. ASOS (www.asos.com) has an amazing selection of midi dresses and that is where I typically buy most of my statement dresses.

Power Suit

I believe that every professional, regardless of your field, should own a suit. You never know when your next opportunity may occur and you always want to be prepared. Being prepared is the entire premise behind having a wardrobe that is fully developed and functional. You will be prepared for any professional or personal occasion that may come your way. Having a go-to suit will ensure that no matter what happens, you will always be ready. A good suit can give you credibility, as strange as that may sound. It says a lot about you and how you carry yourself, particularly if it fits correctly...and It MUST fit correctly.

....

PRO TIP: Have your suit professionally fitted. You can immediately tell when a suit doesn't fit properly. If you're going to spend the money and get a suit, don't do it halfway. Make sure to have the suit professionally tailored so that it fits you perfectly. You can get alterations done at any tailor or even at Nordstrom (www.nordstrom.com). Having the right pieces in your closet is only part of it, making sure that those pieces also fit correctly is equally as important.

....

Find Combinations That Work

There are some color and style combinations that work impeccably well together. One of the biggest tips I can recommend for having a more polished professional look is to use these combinations to your advantage. Dress in color combinations that are flattering for your skin tone, work for you industry, and fit into the image you want to portray.

The most iconic is without a doubt black and white. Black and white is a color combination that instantly looks chic and effortless. Navy blue and grey also look very professional together. If you work in a corporate setting I recommend neutrals as the basis for your outfits, then using brighter colors as accent.

PRO TIP: Buy black blazers and pants together so that they match perfectly. This is one of the best pieces of clothing advice I was ever given. Especially if you're like me and find yourself wearing suits a lot, it is important to wear black pieces that are the same tone. In certain light different fabrics, even if they are both black, can look different. Especially if you are purchasing your first suit, buy them in a set.

Different Industry, Different Standard

Depending on your industry the way that you approach dressing for work will vary. However, the one common theme across each industry is that how you dress contributes to your visual identity. Think of yourself as the CEO of your life and how you dress is what others will think of your brand (aka you). The impression that you want to give, regardless of industry, should always be consistent. But the standard for someone like me, who works in the finance industry as a consultant, is very different from someone who works as a technical designer in the fashion industry. Different industries have different standards and learning what that standard is for your particular industry will give you a professional advantage. It all comes back to optics, and knowing how to dress from the start will allow you to consistently meet, and exceed, expectations.

Finance and Banking

Business professional is the standard in the finance and banking worlds and there is typically a strict dress code. Neutral colors such as black, grey, and navy will become your best friends and you will definitely wear a suit at some point. Minimal and simple jewelry is best. This is not the type of environment where you want to have loud or distracting accessories. Your clothes should be ironed and you should look as neat as possible. In these industries what you wear is extremely important to showing credibility. Do not let this intimidate you. Just be sure to do research on your specific company so you know what to expect.

Law and Politics

Business casual is the standard in the world of law and politics, with the occasional need to dress business professional depending on the environment. I remember when I worked as a law clerk I would dress business causal when in the office, typically khakis, blazers, and sweaters. But whenever I had to accompany an attorney to court I always wore a black suit. Blazers will definitely be an important part of your wardrobe. Neutrals are definitely still worn but you can add more color and personality to your clothing in these industries. Again, researching the specific firm that you will be at is key. Company websites are usually a great place to start just to get a feel for the office culture.

Creative and Fashion

Creative fields are a place where showing your personal style is necessary and often encouraged. Thinking outside the box is the norm and the same goes for your clothing as well. Play around with different trends and colors, this is an environment where your image is an amazing form of self-expression. Build upon the basics but let your creativity show. If you're going for an interview I recommend looking at the company website to get an idea of how others dress.

Retail

For jobs in retail you can definitely show your own personal style. Different stores have different dress codes and uniforms so what you wear will vary depending on the store. Regardless of the uniform, it is all about adding your own personal touch and looking as neat as possible. I worked retail for a semester at City Sports while I was in college. Even though I was required to wear a company t-shirt I always made sure it was wrinkle free and that I wore cool sneakers to go with the look. Whatever you have to wear to work, make it your own. If you're interviewing for a retail position I recommend business casual. You can't go wrong with a blazer paired with khakis or jeans.

Tech

Current tech culture is definitely more relaxed than business casual. Jeans, t-shirts, and sneakers are very common in this industry but I have also seen business casual in tech offices as well. If you're interviewing with a tech company, I recommend dressing business casual unless they explicitly say otherwise. Once you are hired then you can dress more casual depending on the office. But when starting out, you want your first impression to be a positive one that portrays the right message.

Teaching

Teaching is a broad field with many different standards of dress depending on your school, grade level, and position. In general though, the teaching field is predominantly business casual with the ability to show your personal style as well. Khakis, sweaters, and bright statement pieces will help to add personality to your teaching wardrobe. Regardless of the grade you teach, looking neat and put together will leave a good impression.

Fashion Role Model

Is there someone whose style you have always admired or someone whose closet you dream of one day having? Just like in business where having a mentor to help guide your career is incredibly useful, so are fashion role models. This can be anyone but particularly someone who works in a similar field or a field where you see yourself. I'm not saying you have to copy exactly piece for piece the styles of your fashion role model, but use them as a bench mark then add your own twist. When you see others being and looking their best, it inspires you to do the same. I've found that you have to stay inspired and having women who you can relate to both professionally and fashionably is incredibly motivating. What are the top women in your field wearing? Maybe you love what they're wearing or maybe you want to change it and add your own style. The point is to recognize that there are infinite possibilities when it comes to finding inspiration on dressing for success.

ACTION ITEM: In the notes section of this book, write down the top 5 people whose style best represents how you want to dress for work and life. Anyone that comes to mind whose style or career you admire. Refer back to this list whenever you need inspiration.

Having constant inspiration is an amazing way to find great looks and to stay inspired. One tool that I have found helps me to find inspiration is Pinterest (www.pinterest.com). Pinterest is an amazing platform that is full of endless amounts of style inspiration. I have an entire Pinterest board dedicated to style that includes different looks I hope to one day try. If you're a visual person like me, making a Pinterest board dedicated to looks you want to try for work will be very helpful as you think about building your closet and image. I also recommend following inspiring people on all of your social media, including Instagram, so that you are constantly surrounded by great examples of how to dress.

Chapter 4: Dress for the Job
Summary

....

The Difference between Business Professional and Business Casual

Key Pieces for Any Professional Wardrobe

- Blazer
- Pencil Skirt
- Statement Coat
- Sweaters, Blouses, and Shirts
- The Little Black Dress
- Power Suit

Find Combinations that Work

Different Industry, Different Standard

Fashion Role Model

CHAPTER 5

CONFIDENCE

Go confidently in the direction of your dreams

...Live the life you've imagined

-Henry David Thoreau

This is my favorite quote and has been my motto ever since starting Styled by Olivia. Everyone deserves to live their best life and a huge part of that is confidence, not just in yourself, but in life. And for me, part of that confidence has come from my style. I know who I am and what I stand for, which has allowed me to have fun with my style and dress in a way that truly reflects who I am. Confidence is one of the most important aspects of looking and feeling your best. When you look good you feel good, and the positive energy and confidence you exude will translate to your work, regardless of your professional environment.

Mindset Matters

Your mindset matters. The thoughts you have every single day are what shape your attitude and your life. I love the quote, "Attitude is the difference between an ordeal and an adventure" because it is so incredibly true. If you wake up every single day telling yourself that you look bad or don't fit in at your office or that your life sucks, then it will. I've been there. It is so easy to get down on yourself and only focus on the negatives. But you can't concentrate on what's going wrong. You have to tell yourself every day that you can do this. You can change the way you dress, your mindset, and your life if you're willing to shift the way that you think. You have to change your mindset in order to not only look your best, but to transform your life.

Anyone who knows me now would find it very hard to believe that I used to really struggle with my self-esteem all throughout high school and college. I never thought I was pretty enough, good enough, smart enough (you get the idea). Having that kind of attitude really held me back and stopped me from reaching my true potential. It wasn't until I started Styled by Olivia back in 2014 (from my college dorm room) that I really started to shift the way I was thinking about myself and it completely changed my life. After years of having people compliment my style and ask me for advice on professional attire, it finally clicked that my passion for styling was not an accident and I needed to stop hiding it. So not only did my perspective change, consequently my work changed too. I was more confident in my abilities and I found my voice. I knew that regardless of the situations I encountered professionally, there was always a way for me to add value. That realization helped to solidify my confidence in myself professionally and has helped me to get to where I am today. You have to be confident in who you are and what you know. There is a reason you have made it this far in your career and you have so much to give. Where ever you decide to work, you are so valuable and they are lucky to have you.

You are Amazing

You are amazing, in case anyone hasn't told you recently, and that fact should inspire you. Regardless of what you are wearing, you are fabulous. And until you really understand and internalize that, you will not truly look your best. Ultimately who you are as a person and the type of work that you do will speak volumes when it comes to your professional career. The optics and looking your best is only part of the battle. Belief in yourself is the other. Confidence is defined as the feeling of self-assurance arising from one's appreciation of one's own abilities or qualities. You have to really appreciate where you are at right now and believe in yourself as a person.

Be Patient with Yourself

I know from experience that when it comes to confidence it is so much easier said than done. It takes time and you have to be patient with yourself. Confidence is not something that can be bought or attained overnight. I could style every outfit that you wear and dress you for your dream job. But unless you believe in yourself and believe how amazing you are, it does not matter what you are wearing, you will not feel your best. I used to tear myself apart for any and every *perceived* flaw that I had and make myself feel horrible about myself. Why? I really didn't think I was that great. I was insecure and I let all of my negative thoughts control my actions. But what I started to do was fake it. I would *act* like I knew what I was doing and that I was 100 percent confident in myself, until one day I actually was that confident. But it took time and it was incredibly uncomfortable. I'm not going to glamorize it and say that everything was perfect and I just overtime flawlessly transitioned and became the person I am today. Wrong. I had to fight to become the woman I am today. I think because this is the era of social media where everyone's life looks perfect online, many of us do not see the struggle and the work that truly goes on behind the scenes. I had to put in serious work, not just on my closet but on myself. I had to fail. I had to not get the internship or job of my dreams. I had to be told no. I had to be turned down multiple times in order to get to the place I'm at today. It was not flawless and I felt like a hotmess for most of it, but the growth and transformation I experienced was invaluable.

Now, I can walk into any interview or business meeting and know what I bring to the table and command respect.

That type of confidence and belief in oneself is the greatest thing you could ever wear. Act like you have all of the confidence in the world and see how your life changes. It's not easy and you will have to work at it every single day. But be patient with yourself. Being able to truly own who you are and what you are about will completely change the way you approach your job and your life.

In today's ever changing professional world, life is already tough enough without having to constantly worry about what to wear. The struggle is real but getting dressed doesn't have to be. Looking put together in any situation should be second nature, and with the tools in this book it can be. Cultivating a functional wardrobe that helps you to effortlessly look your best will allow you to focus all of your energy on building your career, while naturally exuding confidence. Feeling and looking your best truly is a key part of building a powerful visual identity and making lasting impressions. But it all starts from within and with belief in yourself. Close your eyes and picture yourself at your dream job in the best outfit you can imagine.

Now open your eyes and realize that the vision you have of yourself is exactly who you are today. You are already that person and once you understand that, you will begin to make your vision a reality.

Resources

Below is a list of the resources mentioned throughout the book. This list is constantly changing and growing so to keep up with the latest information visit www.styledbyolivia.com.

Downloads and More Information

www.styledbyolivia.com/about

www.styledbyolivia.com/giveback

www.styledbyolivia.com/shop

Where to Buy Closet Organization

The Container Store: www.containerstore.com

IKEA: www.ikea.com

Target: www.target.com

Organizations to Donate Clothing

Dress for Success: www.dressforsuccess.org

Good Will: www.goodwill.org/donate-and-shop

Salvation Army: www.satruck.org

Resources

Stores Mentioned

ASOS: www.asos.com

Buffalo Exchange: www.buffaloexchange.com

Century 21: www.c21stores.com

Fashionphile: www.fashionphile.com

LOFT: www.loft.com

Nordstrom: www.nordstrom.com

Nordstrom Rack: www.nordstromrack.com

Plato's Closet: www.platoscloset.com

TJMaxx: www.tjmaxx.tjx.com

Zara: www.zara.com

Acknowledgements

First and foremost I have to thank God. I cannot thank Him enough for constantly working in my life and giving me the vision and strength to write this book. My goal has always been to share what I've learned through my career to help inspire women to look and feel their best. I'm so grateful that I'm able to accomplish that and live my purpose through this book. This was not an easy task and I am so thankful to everyone that made this book possible. Huge thank you to my incredible sister Rachel Montague for her constant support and design expertise, this book would not have been written without you. I also owe a huge thank you to the amazing Sarindee Wickramasuriya for all of her support, generosity, and always being there me throughout the writing process. And thank you to Osato Aibangbee for her constant inspiration and for always encouraging me to reach my potential.

Philippians 4:13

NOTES

NOTES

NOTES